I0087710

CAREER BOOK 5
16 Career-readiness Strategies
for Parents
of New Job Finders
With Special Needs

JIM HASSE

DEDICATION

To my dad, Laverne,
who taught his family by example
that spearheading innovation in school, church and small business
can be personally both frustrating and fulfilling.

CONTENTS

Growing in Self-confidence

Discovering Disability's Competitive Advantage

ACKNOWLEDGMENTS

A special thank you to Peter Altschul, Fernando Botelho, Earl Brancel, Judy Ettinger, Floyd Harris, Pam Hasse, Nan Hawthorne, Mary Krohn, Nancy O'Connell, Liz Seger, Ruth-Ellen Simmonds, Don Storhoff, Mårten Tegnestam and Bob Williams – all of whom (among many others) have provided me with valuable guidance during critical moments in my career development.

WHAT I BELIEVE

Over the last 20 years, I have identified a range of time-tested strategies I believe parents can use to prepare youngsters with disabilities for the world of work.

I believe guiding parents in implementing these strategies on a wide scale will bring these two results:

- More people with disabilities will be ready for work.
- Employers will find more job candidates with disabilities who they consider qualified for open jobs.

That's why I seek non-profit and corporate partners which have wide, established connections with parents who are looking for the answers I can provide about how to help their youngsters with special needs prepare for meaningful careers.

My message: I believe people can put disability to work as a competitive edge in today's job market.

For a long time, those of us dealing with disability employment issues have realized that individuals with a disability can add a valuable perspective to corporate efforts in the mainstream business world.

That message has had a difficult time getting public attention, but that may be changing.

I believe we can now more confidently state this finding: Employees with disabilities are more likely to bring drive, focus and innovation to the workplace than their non-disabled counterparts.

Consider the following three contemporary authors who have recently brought those three "advantages" of disability employment to the public's attention through books which have received good reviews in the mainstream media.

First, in "The Triple Package: What Really Determines Success" (2014), Amy Chua and Jed Rubenfeld discuss the reasons behind personal achievement.

Successful people, they say, tend to feel simultaneously inadequate and superior. They:

1. Believe they are, in some ways, exceptional.
2. Are insecure about their worth or place in society – that they're not "good enough."
3. Resist the temptation to give up instead of persevering in the face of difficult circumstances.

They may appear to have a chip on their shoulders because they have a need to prove themselves.

For those of us with a disability, for instance, we may have a personal need to prove to others that we are the "exception" to commonly held beliefs within our society about people with disabilities in general.

I believe that inadequate/superior package tends to generate a personal drive in "overachieving" individuals with a disability – a need to prove oneself by sacrificing present gratification in pursuit of future attainment.

I must confess that this inadequate/superior duality fits me to a tee. For a thorough examination of that duality in me, go to the directory for my series of seven Amazon books about my personal transformation stories as a person with cerebral palsy at cerebral-palsy-career-builders.com/transformation-stories.html.

Second, Geoff Colvin sums up the power of deliberate practice with a purpose in his book, "Talent Is Overrated: What Really Separates World-Class Performers from Everybody Else" (2010). He writes:

"...The most important effect of practice in great performers is
that it takes them beyond -- or, more precisely, around – the
limitations most of us think of as critical."

He pinpoints exactly why I believe it makes good business sense
to hire people with disabilities who have developed the motivation to
work hard at precisely the things they need to improve so they can
contribute to a company's bottom line.

Colvin cites research that indicates what we think of as "innate
talent" is more accurately termed "long-term, sustained practice at
what really counts" driven by a passion to reach a goal (or in
response to the triple package described above by Amy Chua and Jed
Rubenfeld). In other words, Colvin says it's all about self-discipline
no matter what the motivation.

Third, in "David and Goliath: Underdogs, Misfits and the Art of
Battling Giants" (2013), Malcolm Gladwell offers a new
interpretation of what it means to live well with a disability.

His main point: What is innovative, beautiful and important in
the world often arises from what looks like suffering and adversity.

In other words, being an underdog can change people. "It can
open doors and create opportunities and educate and enlighten and
make possible what otherwise may seem unthinkable," Gladwell
writes.

Gladwell even promotes the idea of a "desirable difficulty," such
as dyslexia, a learning disability that causes much frustration for
students as they learn how to read but, at the same time, forces them
to compensate for that barrier by developing better listening and
problem-solving skills – and by being innovative.

I encourage you, as a parent, to keep these considerations in
mind as you help your youngster with special needs prepare for a
meaningful job in an integrated work situation.

I researched and wrote the material for this book long before the
afore-mentioned authors became popular. Over the last 20 years, I
have gradually realized the importance of disability as the foundation
for the resiliency of humankind throughout history.

However, only in the last five years have I publicly admitted that my disabilities, while they have made life tougher for me to live, have also, within certain contexts, become an aggregate advantage for me.

That reconciliation – and even love – of one's personal vulnerabilities perhaps come with age and the advantage of hindsight.

At any rate, please keep these initial remarks in mind as you review the following career-readiness strategies for your youngster. Your youngster's personal circumstances as well as the National Career Development Guidelines in the back of this book can also temper your thoughts.

Will your youngster be able to frame disability in such a way when he or she makes the transition from school to work that will help hiring managers recognize disability's competitive advantage?

Will those hiring managers seize the opportunity they have for boosting drive, focus and innovation in their workplaces by hiring your son or daughter?

I believe the answer to both of those questions can be "yes."

But, first things first. Your youngster needs to first grow in self-confidence.

STRATEGY 1 – RECOGNIZE
THE IMPORTANCE OF MOTIVATION

A job seeker with special needs must be highly motivated to work around accessibility barriers (particularly those which involve transportation and adaptive technology issues) that may be standing in the way of getting hired.

You can help your mentee turn such barriers into career builders by showing what it's like to be nimble in resolving such issues.

A nimble and solution-oriented job seeker who is willing to take personal responsibility for tackling tough on-the-job accessibility issues shows employers that he or she:

- **Prefers** to be as independent as possible in gaining workable accommodations.
- **Realizes** it's a personal responsibility to become technologically savvy.
- **Knows** how to manage problems in a variety of settings at work and at home.
- **Is willing** to set priorities and work toward long-term goals.

That's why I stress that personal motivation is a key factor in an individual's career development.

As your youngster gains experience in volunteer and part-time jobs while in school, you'll soon realize that he or she can transfer those attitudes and attributes to concrete business situations -- accomplishments that can be highlighted on resumes. That's a mark of maturity.

Here are some comments that I have collected over the last few years from individuals with a disability who are today working in the mainstream job market. I believe they have succeeded in working around disability employment barriers largely because they have demonstrated their maturity in tackling the on-the-job accessibility issues they each face.

On a personal level, they know the importance of motivation in working around real and perceived barriers.

Let's hear the advice they have for your soon-to-be employed young son or daughter.

David:

"People are hired because they have shown that they can get the job done. If we can't do that, for any reason, then we can't be hired and retained as valuable business assets...

"...With my employer, I was simply moved to a project that features accessible technologies that work with JAWS...

"I am considering myself very lucky that I have an employer who sees the value I add to the company and does not simply throw me away because of my technology inaccessibility problems...

"...I am very rarely late to work and, on the few occasions when it has happened, it hasn't been repeated in a very long time. I believe the reasons for the good service I receive on paratransit have a lot to do with my proactive advocacy efforts. I simply refuse to accept rudeness and unprofessionalism, and I always insist on prompt resolution of all issues, escalating through the chain of command until proper action is ultimately taken.

"...When you take the initiative and act for yourself, you show the world that you are personally motivated and have what it takes to effectively perform the duties of that job you seek!"

Nancy:

"...I have had several jobs and have done well in most. In some cases, I got along with minimal accommodation, but more recently I did receive the basic tools I needed. Still, I have preferred what I was able to choose for myself... The impact on my family's credit cards notwithstanding, I feel the independence has been well worth it...

"What I have done about needing transportation for my business is simply gone entirely online. I train via the phone. All meetings are via chat or messenger. I have a knack for making this not look like a disadvantage but rather a distinction..."

Kathy:

"...We all know that we have to use whatever is at our disposal to be viable in today's job market. Knowing as much technology as you can is a real plus."

John:

"...I'm always amused when I look back at the situations I resolved at work --- issues my co-workers without disabilities didn't have to think about...

"I do know that getting a job and developing my career was the key to everything else I wanted to accomplish..."

Some adjectives come to mind as I review these snippets: realistic, savvy, grateful, proactive, assertive, creative, independent, and accomplished.

Aren't those some of the personal attributes you want your son or daughter to show prospective employers? They are the mark of maturity and self-confidence-- a quality hiring managers seek in the job candidates they interview. They also remind us about the importance of motivation.

Your young man or woman can demonstrate maturity during job interviews by being savvy (and helpful) about the on-the-job accommodations he or she needs.

To do so, I recommend following these three steps toward becoming "adaptive technology" independent:

- **Become** familiar and stay up-to-date with the resources on the Job Accommodations Network (JAN) that apply to a specific situation.
- **Form** a rotating, informal team of "experts" from your local area who can keep your young man or woman up-to-date on a routine basis about which cutting-edge technologies can work best to meet personal needs at a cost that is not prohibitive.
- **Work** with your state vocational rehabilitation office to see what funding is available for obtaining needed adaptive technology.

Can you picture your son or daughter managing those resources and that informal adaptive technology team? That experience itself is worthy to note on a resume.

It all stems from recognizing the importance of motivation, the impact motivation has on self-confidence and the value motivation has in today's job market.

STRATEGY 2 – CONCENTRATE ON FOUR BASIC SKILLS

 A s both a job seeker and hiring manager for more than three decades, I've found that there are essentially four basic skills which can determine how successful a job candidate will be in landing a meaningful job. Those four basic skills are: marketing, advocating, problem solving and negotiating.

Let me briefly explain my personal guidelines for developing those four basic skills.

Marketing

A huckster sells or promotes in an aggressive and flashy manner. A job seeker does not need to be a huckster.

But, your new job seeker can't ignore personal marketing and personal branding, either. In today's American culture, which puts a premium on individuality, a job seeker needs to identify his or her strengths and passion and develop a personal brand which showcases them in an effective, sincere manner.

Help your new job seeker to be objective about what he or she can offer employers in the light of disability. The trick is to then offer those attributes in a forthright presentation which puts the employer first and your son or daughter second.

My recommendation: Replace the "objective" portion (which is "me" oriented) of a resume with an "offering statement," which, in one sentence, tells prospective employers what your job seeker can do for them.

An offering statement is brief, reflecting your job seeker's well-selected accomplishments and skills. Employers are more interested in what your job seeker has to offer than what his or her personal objectives are.

An effective offering statement is the culmination of much reflection and hard work, even though it's preferably only one or two sentences long.

A good offering statement can drive your job seeker's entire job marketing campaign.

Advocating

Naked self-promotion has a negative connotation in business circles, where what's good for the company or organization is paramount. But self-advocacy, starting with a solid understanding of both what your job seeker can do for a potential employer and what tools he or she needs to do the job, is vital.

So, help your job seeker practice leveling with prospective employers, saying, in essence, "This is what I need to do an effective job for you, and here's how I can help you get what I need at a reasonable cost and at not a lot of time on your part." In other words, your new job seeker needs to be a self-advocate with the authenticity valued in today's business world.

At no time should a job seeker with a disability beg for a job by falling back on the cliché of "all I need is just one break."

My counseling principle: Your job seeker with special needs must make his or her own breaks by effectively preparing for a job, mastering effective job marketing techniques and pointing out to targeted employers why he or she is the best person for a particular job.

Problem Solving

Imagination and daydreaming are fine pastimes, but what counts in business is applied creativity. Everyone can be creative, but not everyone is adept at applying creativity to personal challenges or on-the-job situations.

Problem solving is the ability to tap creativity for relieving a pain or paving the way to a gain -- either on a personal level or within a corporate setting.

Your job seeker needs to demonstrate problem-solving ability in both areas, if possible. For instance, maybe your son or daughter can show how he or she has harnessed technology to live well with a disability. How can that same ingenuity be used in a workplace environment and help a company take advantage of often unseen opportunities?

The more specific your job seeker can get in this regard the better. Having the demonstrative ability to find the right match between need and solution will give him or her the self-confidence for competing effectively in today's job market.

That may seem like a tough guidance counseling principle, but let me explain.

My guidance counseling principle: Encourage your new job seeker to use brief stories to trace the evolution of his or her problem-solving abilities – and trace that evolution, if possible, to what he or she has learned as a result of effectively coping with a disability.

Negotiating

Instead of approaching an employment opportunity as an underdog due to a perceived weakness (either as a personal perception or a false assumption on the part of a prospective employer), your new job seeker needs to develop negotiating skills designed to approach decisions about employment conditions, benefits and salary from a position of strength.

After all, as a job candidate, your son or daughter is selling his or her skills, experience and attributes, and the prospective employer is buying them.

Although I think I have an ample measure of self-esteem and a long history of success in the mainstream job market, I find that I sometimes miss opportunities to effectively negotiate terms of an arrangement that could be even more beneficial to me. I often overlook the critical dynamics of a situation. I don't take my own guidance counseling advice.

Maybe it's because I'm frequently so involved in what I can do in sidestepping personal obstacles associated with my disability that I get preoccupied by the "big picture" of what is happening and forget about tying up the details in my favor.

That just happened recently when my wife, Pam, and I leased a new car. We thought we had the deal tied up by telephone before we got to the dealership, but then our favorite color was not available except on a "demonstrator" and that threw a new set of figures at me. I missed an opportunity to further negotiate in the light of these new factors.

My guidance counseling recommendation: Encourage your new job finder to take courses in negotiation, read books about negotiation and practice negotiating skills. Knowing (and demonstrating) how to negotiate effectively for what he or she wants, needs and deserves in terms of salary, benefits and accommodations will make your son or daughter a stronger job candidate and a more effective employee.

Help your new job finder cultivate these four basic skills: marketing, advocating, problem solving and negotiating. Each is a confidence builder.

STRATEGY 3 – BUILD
A PERSONAL BRAND

I think a personal brand is especially important for job seekers with special needs because it helps them and their potential employers to realistically answer these three questions:

- **Will your every-day tasks** tap and stretch your key strengths as a new employee?
- **Will your new job** motivate you because you'll be carrying out tasks you love to do?
- **Will your disability** really matter in carrying out the duties of the job at hand?

Developing a personal brand is a strategy for taking ownership of one's uniqueness in a world that is too often glitzy but bland. Finding the best opportunities for reaching one's full potential is usually a gradual journey.

The concept started with executives in the 1960s but became popular in the late 1990s when business author and speaker Tom Peters became one of its most famous evangelists.

Susan Chritton, author of "Personal Branding for DUMMIES," writes that branding oneself is no longer an option (it's a necessity) for individuals who are serious about managing their careers.

In this new economy, she points out, companies are developing more project-based work (within and outside of the work site), assigning full-time employees to work with temporary workers.

That means your college student is entering a workplace where there's more employee turnover and needs to be known by what he or she can do (not by a job title). That calls for a personal brand which is portable, constant and recognizable wherever work carries an individual.

I believe just-out-of-school job seekers need to register their personal names as a dot com domain and build a simple web site where they explain who they are and what they offer prospective employers. That's the beginning of creating a personal brand.

Encourage the young son or daughter you're coaching to take these three simple steps.

- **First**, do a whois.com search to see if the version of your name (full name, nickname first initials with last name etc.) you use most often to identify yourself is available as a domain name for your site.
- **Second**, once you have settled on a domain name that includes some form of your proper name, always use that proper name version in identifying yourself on anything you write for publication, in your social media profiles, on your resumes, in your portfolio, e-mail sig etc. Branding consistency is the key.
- For an example, see my personal web site at jimhasse.com. JRH.com (my initials) had already been taken when I launched my personal web site in 2010.
- **Third**, you can use a domain hosting service such as godaddy.com to register your domain name and build a simple, not-costly web site like I did. Your site can display your offering statement, your resume, your portfolio etc., and you can set up an e-mail address that is unique to your web site.

Notice I brand myself as a *"disability employment expert who helps individuals put disability to work as a competitive edge in today's job market."* That's my 15-second elevator pitch, a reply I can use when I'm asked, "What do you do?"

My statement often leads to question in reply: "How do you do that?"

My standard response: *"I walk the people I coach through a series of career builders so they can gain the confidence they need to deal effectively with disability employment issues."*

For those who are really interested in my services, my two simple personal brand statements set the stage for exchanging contact information and for further discussion within a more appropriate venue.

Of course, discovering what I was all about and putting it into two simple sentences did not happen overnight. I've had career coaches and mentors help me in that discovery over many years.

But, now's the time (while your son or daughter with special needs is still making the school- to-work transition) to put in writing answers to these questions: What is your passion? In what situations do you find yourself most comfortable, authentic and likable?

I wish your son or daughter the best in this journey toward building a personal brand. Remember, it takes time. But, it's worth the effort because it's a confidence booster.

STRATEGY 4 – CONSIDER A FUNCTIONAL RESUME

Your son or daughter may have limited part-time working experience as an intern or volunteer, so a chronological or combination resume may not as work well a functional resume.

A functional resume is particularly useful for emphasizing transferrable skills from volunteer or paid work or coursework for those who are new graduates, who have limited experience or who do not want to call attention to their age.

The following sample functional resume (one that highlights work results instead of a chronological work history) happens to be my own – one that is based on my personal definition of success.

Before building that framework, I recognized, after some soul searching, that I'm "accomplishment motivated." In other words, I feel successful when I know I've completed a task, and that task was done well.

That understanding helped me identify my most important workplace accomplishments and the key success factors within those accomplishments which would likely drive my future achievements.

"Accomplishments" and "key success factors" were the key elements I used in building my functional resume.

Here's how I took my critical first steps in building the framework for my current resume -- a framework I started developing in 1993.

Identifying my "Key Success Factors"

I used the following eight steps to examine my work experience, review my accomplishments and identify my key success factors -- an essential, initial exercise before I developed my resume and charted a path to my next career position.

1. **Listed** my functional experiences on the job as well as in volunteer positions.
2. **Identified** three to five over-arching, key success factors which contributed to the accomplishments I listed as functional experiences in step one.
3. **Defined** briefly what these key success factors meant to me in terms of the individual skills and personal qualities I used to build the accomplishments I listed in step one.
4. **Selected** three to five individual skills/personal qualities from the list in step three which most closely apply to the accomplishments I listed in step one.
5. **Ranked** these five skills/qualities I possess according to how strong they are in me, how useful they've been to me and how enjoyable they've been to me.
6. **Matched** my key success factors I identified in step two with the five skills/qualities I ranked in step five according to strength.
7. **Cited** two specific examples of functional experience I listed in step one to illustrate those key success factors/skills/qualities.
8. **Selected** the best functional experience example of the two in each case.

Building my Resume

Here's how I used my key success factors to build my resume – a sample functional resume that you can recommend as guide for your new job finder:

- I rearranged my key success factors, skills and qualities, putting the most important first, and pruned them from five to four.
- This list identified me as a resource person for defining direction and managing change within an organization. To me, that could be summed up in two words: "Gaining Alignment." "Gaining Alignment" became the "hinge" for putting the pieces of my resume together.
- I now converted my four key success factors, skills and qualities into four key result areas, using action verbs to succinctly describe essential activities involved in each of the functional experience examples I had previously chosen. For each, I then added more concrete results. So I ended up with one page which highlighted my functional experience.
- This one-page statement of my functional experience became the core of my resume, a 17-by-11 sheet of very light gray cover stock folded in half. It became my second page. The fourth page (or backside) of my one-fold pamphlet (resume) I left bank.
- The third page included these four sections: Professional Experience, Education, Professional Affiliations, and Other Commitments.
- I carried the "Gaining Realignment" theme from page two (functional experience) to the front page of my resume by citing a favorite quotation that defined what those two words meant to me.

Here is that quotation:

*"When you identify with your company's purpose,
when you experience ownership in a shared vision,
you find yourself doing your life's work,
instead of just doing time."*

- John Naisbitt
Futurist, author

See how my completed resume looks online and how I tie my experience in learning how to live well with a disability into my success in business.

I now see, 20 years later, that "Gaining Alignment" still works as my two-word statement of my purpose in life. I've been out of the business communications field for two decades, but, as someone who is focused on disability employment issues, I'm now helping job seekers align themselves with the needs of employers -- a different venue but same purpose.

Help your new job finder identify his or her key success factors, workplace skills and personal qualities and convert them into a one-page statement of concrete results wrapped around functional experience.

Your youngster's key search words for resume databases will pop out of his or her statement of functional experience. With those key words as a core, your young job seeker can adapt his or her own functional resume to a wide variety of uses in an effective job marketing campaign.

I can vouch from personal experience that going through that process is a confidence builder.

STRATEGY 5 – DEVELOP
A "GOOD ANSWER" FOR JOB INTERVIEWS

At a recent workshop for updating skills in career development facilitation, I heard two individuals who help technical college students with special needs develop career management skills concur on this observation:

> "We don't know where this comes from, but we find students with disabilities generally have some catching up to do (compared to the general student population) when it comes to gaining self-confidence and knowing how to sell themselves to employers as viable job candidates."

I was not surprised to hear two in-the-trenches people actually question why students with disabilities have difficulty "selling themselves" in this age of self-promotion.

After all, turning disability into a positive in the eyes of an employer requires reflection, insight and extra work. It's one of the keys to gaining self-confidence.

Here are a couple of extra questions non-disabled job candidates usually don't have to ask themselves as they develop their job marketing programs:

- **"How do** I gather enough self-esteem to look at my disability as a strength instead of a weakness?
- **"How do** I describe that strength in a way that is meaningful to a prospective employer?"
- **"How do** I get that whole disability issue out of the way first during a job interview so I can then focus on my strengths for the job at hand?"

Tell your new job seeker:

> "That kind of preparation for a job hunt is well worth the extra effort. It's part of the process for gaining self-confidence, which you've been working on since you've been a child."

The keys to getting it done are introspection, perception and projection. Again, that requires work.

Debra L. Angel and Elizabeth E. Harney are authors of "No One is Unemployable: Creative Solutions for Overcoming Barriers to Employment."

Here are their responses (in capsule form) to the three questions above for your new job seeker:

> Develop a "good answer" for a reply to questions about your disability and your ability to do a job; plant it in the back of your mind in case you need to use it -- something short and sweet that comes off the tip of your tongue naturally during a job interview.

What Makes a "Good Answer"?

Ideally, your new job seeker's "good answer" can act as a transition from talking about disability to describing his or her work skills during job interviews so the interviewer can focus instead on what your youngster can offer the company or organization.

To develop a "good answer" to a real and/or perceived disability barrier to employment, the authors first ask a job seeker to consider these two questions:

- "**How do** you perceive the barrier to your employment?"
- "**How do** you think the employer perceives that same barrier?"

To find the key to your youngster's "good answer," the authors suggest that both of you (mentor and mentee) search for reasons why the barrier should no longer concern the employer.

Can the barrier be used to further qualify your youngster for a particular job? Or, has overcoming the barrier helped your son or daughter develop skills or knowledge that a prospective employer needs (such as resourcefulness, problem solving, planning or persistence)?

By personally developing a "good answer," your young job seeker can minimize fear of job interviews and exhibit more self-confidence because he or she will begin to see the whole job search process in a more positive light.

STRATEGY 6 –PREPARE
FOR TRICKY INTERVIEW QUESTIONS

As a hiring manager myself during the late 1970s to early 1990s, I conducted job interviews to staff my small department with professionals as well as summer college interns and part-time high school support people.

Here are three job interview questions (and the answers I wanted to hear) that I used quite frequently. I must admit that, from today's perspective, they may have been "tricky" (designed to weed out candidates who looked good on paper but didn't fit my department's "culture").

Where would you *really* like to work?

I didn't want to hear the name of another company or organization or another location. Our central office at the time was in a rural area, and my antenna were up for job candidates who considered the job opportunity I was offering as, in their view, second or third options due to the location.

What I really wanted to hear was this: "This is where I want to work, and this job is what I want to do."

Can you describe how you solved a work problem?

This is the most basic of job interview questions, so top job candidates should always be prepared with a ready answer.

Yet, all too often my interviewees either couldn't come up with something on the spot or missed the opportunity to highlight their best skills and attributes. Either way, as an interviewer, I was learning how the individual's mind worked and how well that person was prepared for the interview.

My advice for your new job seeker: Have an answer ready -- like how you resolved a time management issue to take on a special assignment. Or, better yet, tie your answer to how you learned to work around a problem presented by the fact you have a disability (such as finding an accommodation while in school at very little cost).

In other words, showcase a unique achievement.

Can you describe a time when you messed up?

This is one of those job interview questions that really is a trap for your young job finder, if he or she is not prepared for it.

One question within that question is whether your job finder learns from mistakes or keeps repeating the same errors.

On the other hand, I used this question mainly to discover a job candidate's level of self-confidence. If your youngster would answer this question by providing a list of all of his or her negative attributes, then I'd wonder about his or her insecurities and would not offer the job.

So, coach your new job finder to avoid skirting the issue or making him or herself look bad. Instead, your son or daughter under this situation needs to only briefly mention a single, small, well-intentioned goof and follow up with an important lesson learned from that experience.

Of course, this doesn't deplete the job interview questions that are potential "job killers" for your new job finder, but, in most cases, such difficulties can be avoided through company research, personal branding and interview practice.

My belief is that knowing about the employer, knowing who are and knowing what works and what doesn't during an interview is more important in building your young job finder's self-confidence than simply trying to anticipate tricky interview questions.

STRATEGY 7 – MAKE THE MOST OF THESE THREE CAREER BUILDERS

Based on my personal experience, I'd rank these three topics near the top of my "critical things to do," if I were about to make the big transition from school to work.

- Networking effectively.
- Targeting companies.
- Dressing well.

Let's look at each one of these career builders.

Networking Effectively

Bettina Seidman is a well-known career management coach who has a private practice in Manhattan. She founded SEIDBET Associates in 1990 after a 20-year career in human resources management.

Seidman provides career counseling and professional coaching services to individuals and organizations in the corporate and non-profit sectors. She works with her clients as a thinking partner, providing career and job-transition counseling services such as assessment, goal setting, networking tactics, resume development, and interviewing and negotiating strategies.

Networking, Seidman says, can prove to be highly successful if it's faithfully carried out in a persistent and consistent manner. That's an observation you might want to pass along to your new job seeker.

In her networking scenario, the first step is to develop what she calls an "A" contact list of decision makers who already know you. "Contact them by phone, e-mail or social media," she says, "and ask who they know in your targeted field. Don't ask for a job. That's a turnoff. It puts pressure on them."

Instead of asking for a job, Seidman urges, ask about information and the network they have. To do that effectively, she recommends developing an informal script which tells what type of work your new job seeker wants to do.

"Don't expect 'A' list contacts to have their network information readily available," she cautions. "Instead, tell them you'll get back to them in three or four days for this information: name, title, address, office phone, LinkedIn.com address and e-mail. Since these are business contacts, don't ask for cell phone numbers."

The information your youngster collects by dialoguing with the "A" contact list, Seidman explains, becomes his or her "B" contact list -- people he or she doesn't know but could be helpful in a job search.

Study this "B" list, and then decide who, out of that group, could benefit you the most, if you were introduced to them through LinkedIn.com, says Seidman.

Responding effectively to an online introduction requires a second script that your new job seeker needs to write: a very short pitch about two minutes long which describes his or her career goal, experience, skills, accomplishments and education, she says.

"Put your pitch into a conversational style so you can use it to follow up on your online introduction through a telephone call as well as during job interviews and during in-person networking meetings," Seidman recommends.

Your new job seeker also needs to develop a list of questions to ask during networking or informational meetings with the contacts on the "B" list.

"Don't ask for a job," cautions Seidman. "Instead ask: What do you do? What advice do you have? How did you do this or that? What did you learn?"

Using that technique, job leads will come your way, she maintains.

According to Seidman, executive search firms, on the other hand, yield low job search results for most people. Such firms usually concentrate on jobs with salaries $150,000 and above. Those in that job bracket, she notes, can send a template letter to 10 to 20 firms and follow up in a couple of weeks as part of their job search campaigns.

She said job finders need to realize that they are not the clients of executive search firms. "They work on commission for companies," she points out. "You are not the client. Be careful what you tell them."

There is no online directory for executive search firms, but "Candidate Directory of Executive Search Firms" is available in print.

Targeting Companies

"Submitting resumes online in response to job postings without a targeted approach is the worst way to search for a job," Seidman maintains.

She recommends spending no more than two hours a week in searching and responding to job postings. For those who do, "Weddle's 2013-14 Guide to Employment Sites on the Internet" may prove helpful, she says. Use that guide to write customized letters, she advises, bulleting the skills sought in postings. Then follow up in five days.

Seidman offers what she believes is a better option instead: "Target companies you're interested in with a resume and cover letter and envelope on matching white bond paper. Include a summary of your skills instead of an 'objective.' Never include, 'references upon request' because references are the last step in obtaining a job."

I believe that tactic could be effective, since your son or daughter will stand out by using snail mail and avoiding the electronic glut. I'd use LinkedIn.com to try to get the name of the person most likely to have hiring authority within the department of the company your new job seeker is targeting.

Dressing Well

My sister, Mary, a medical technologist back in 1970s who eventually became manager of a major paper mill, reminded me recently that I once said I thought it was important for me to be well dressed and well groomed as I made the school-to-work transition as an individual with a disability.

I may have been a little obsessed about how I looked, but, on hindsight, that probably served me well because "looking good" gave me self-confidence, raised my credibility among my co-workers and maybe helped people look beyond my disability.

And, I still believe the old rule-of-thumb for those still "green" on the job: "Dress for the job you want – not the one you have right now."

Yet, finding quality, professional, stylish and functional clothing that fits properly and maybe hides the fact the your new job seeker has a spinal curvature or one leg shorter than the other or uses a wheelchair or crutches can be a challenge.

I use a button hook to button the top button of my dress shirts and clip-on ties (which work well if selected carefully). Back in the 1980s, I was able to buy personalized, made-to-fit suits, sports coats and trousers (and even dress shirts) at reasonable prices but not anymore.

Instead, I see two things happening:

- **Scanners** and computer-aided design are making customized clothing more available for people with disabilities.
- **Fashion** designers are starting to serve the disability market. Note the work of Ruth J. Clark, founder of Fashion Moves Inclusive Designs.

Of course, there are many more confidence builders which can determine how successful your new job seeker is in getting that first out-of-school job, but these three are important steps toward breaking into the mainstream job market.

STRATEGY 8 – NETWORK WITHIN TARGETED COMPANIES

Getting hired essentially involves establishing a personal relationship with one's future supervisor based on mutual respect and dignity.

As a job seeker, your son or daughter with special needs never wants to be in a position where he or she appears to be begging to be considered as a job candidate or to get hired. To avoid that kind of sinkhole, your new job seeker needs to learn how to effectively build a network of contacts within targeted companies – contacts who represent an informal online job market because they are the first to know about new openings within their workplaces.

Why LinkedIn Is Important for your Job Finder

That's where LinkedIn can help. It's an excellent tool for doing company research, building a network of contacts and receiving early announcements of online jobs.

I'm always surprised about how many new college graduates are not actively involved on LinkedIn, where open jobs on not always formally posted but, instead are part of the online jobs market that relies on word of mouth. Being actively involved on LinkedIn can definitely build your son or daughter's self-confidence when it comes to finding the right job.

Most of the jobs mentioned on LinkedIn are "go-to-work" type positions. But, if your young job seeker is really looking for online jobs, involving work that can be done from home, LinkedIn is also the place to start because the professionals who congregate on LinkedIn generally offer work-from-home opportunities that are legitimate and are not scams.

To tap into LinkedIn, your new job seeker first needs to use the key words he or she developed as part of personal branding to create a LinkedIn profile. That profile should include fresh stories which illustrate your son or daughter's skills and which are not duplicated on his or her personal website or resume.

Then, at that point, I'd recommend gradually building LinkedIn connections -- connections with people who are really interested in your job seeker and are appropriate for the focus of his or her job search because they are potentially a posting source of online jobs.

Steve Frederick, partner, Frederick Career Services, suggests setting a goal of obtaining 500 solid LinkedIn connections. In doing so, he says, your new job seeker can be considered well connected online and effectively plugged into online jobs announcements for his or her particular job sector. That doesn't happen overnight. It takes time.

How to Use LinkedIn as a Job Finder

Here are six recommendations about how to network within targeted companies from Frederick that you may want to pass along to your new job seeker:

- **Join** and routinely participate in about 12 LinkedIn groups which have strong facilitators who encourage discussion about topics that you find interesting. If you have an article or blog posting that is germane to a particular group's current discussion topic, post a link to your writing in that group. Also watch for discussions of online jobs.
- **Start** your own LinkedIn group, using the keywords from your personal brand in the group's description, if you have time and don't find a group for your particular job search

niche. Differentiate yourself from your competitors, narrow your groups focus and personally invite people to join your group. The people who join your group are valuable contacts in your network as a job seeker because they may be passing along notices about online jobs.

- **Check** new hires for your targeted company. Join the groups they have joined. Establish a mutually beneficial relationship through those groups by congratulating them on their new jobs, talking about their career transitions etc.

- **Search** Google for names of the people you want to contact. That will round out the background you already have about them on LinkedIn. You can even use Google to obtain last names when you only have the last name's initial, if you have the individual's company and title.

- **Obtain** a picture, in LinkedIn Company Search, of the employee longevity of your targeted company, the education level of the workforce, the company's growth, and where current employees previously worked -- all valuable information for deciding whether the company is right for you and whether you want to pursue its online job offerings.

- **Search** for individuals by job type and company in Advanced Search on LinkedIn. You can also search for individuals by the number of LinkedIn connections they have. The cutoff connection number is 500, so those with more than 500 connections show "500+" connections. LinkedIn's networking philosophy is based on a simple rule that says that you should invite to connect only people that you personally know (for instance, school colleagues, co-workers, business partners, service providers etc.).

Frederick suggests that your new job finder set up an RSS feeds, using a tool such as Google Reader, to track answers to questions posed in LinkedIn that may be particularly helpful in networking and job hunting initiatives.

That saves time and provides an opportunity to respond appropriately with a job marketing focus -- again gaining an online presence in specific discussions with hiring managers who may mention openings for online jobs during their discussions.

Another Frederick tip: If your job finder uses RSS, be sure he or she adds secondary e-mail addresses for that purpose for segregating RSS material in the inbox.

All of these features make LinkedIn a terrific tool for your new job finder, who may not be as mobile as other people due to a disability. LinkedIn allows him or her to do quick, easy and methodical company research and keep tabs unpublished job openings.

It's another example of how technology is leveling the playing field in job recruitment for people with special needs. It's a confidence builder.

STRATEGY 9 – USE
THIS PERSONAL DEVELOPMENT TEMPLATE

Encourage your son or daughter to form a "mastermind" group of three to four people for finding answers to key questions related to a job search.

Such a group should ask "what," "how," "when" and "who" (in other words, behavior: "What's the evidence?") -- but not "why."

The group should consist of people who are willing to support one another -- all with one purpose: find meaningful work. If the group can't meet in person, it can meet regularly through telephone conferences, Skype, Google Hangouts, instant messaging, private forums etc.

Here are 10 steps I've used within a mastermind group to evaluate my strengths and weaknesses from a job-hunting perspective. Think about how your job finder can use this template with his or her own mastermind group.

Step One: My Strengths as a Job Seeker

"I've found that I communicate well on paper, that I'm an effective facilitator, and that I'm a strategic thinker."

Step Two: The Three Most Important Strengths

I Can Offer an Employer

"I'm an effective writer, networker and facilitator."

Step Three: My Statement about my Strengths as a Job Seeker

"I develop key connections online within my field because I know how to network effectively in terms of communicating, facilitating, and reciprocating)."

Step Four: How I Can Take Full Advantage of my Strengths

"Since I'm personable and meet people easily, I can become more visible in person to potential employers through volunteer work and in-person networking events."

At this point, I take a different direction with the next four steps. Those next four steps are exactly the same as the first four, but instead of discussing my strengths and how to improve them, I think of the weaknesses (barriers) I face and how I can minimize or work around them.

Step Five: My Barriers as a Job Seeker

"Here are roadblocks I've encountered during my job searches: Procrastination; low attention to detail; low interest in helping prospective employers ramp up for assistive technology I may require at my work station; reluctance to travel independently; low preference for hands-on work."

Step Six: Three Barriers Which Hold Me Back as a Job Seeker

"My three key barriers are a personal avoidance of the responsibility for assistive technology, of hands-on work and of independent travel."

Step Seven: My Statement Describing my Key Barriers

"I won't help you as my employer find assistive technology and travel solutions that I need because I dread getting involved in those details and having to work on it myself."

Step Eight: Ways to Minimize or Eliminate my Key Barriers

"Here are two things I can do to minimize, work around or even eliminate these barriers so I can no longer make my barrier statement (above) truthfully:

"Find a person in my online network who can mentor me about how to work out the details with an employer to obtain the workplace accommodations I need.

"Use my network to locate a person with a similar disability who has learned to travel independently and who is willing to coach me step by step in doing the same."

Step Nine: Factors With the Greatest Effect on my Job Search

"Networking is the one strength I most need to focus on. My one weakness which is the greatest threat to my success as job seeker is accommodations. So, I need to diversify my networking efforts and become an expert about personal workplace accommodations. "

Step Ten: Set a Time Frame for Getting Stronger

"Next Tuesday, I will submit a question on LinkedIn about what it takes to travel independently with my particular disability."

Do you see how following this template can help your new job seeker build a sense of self-confidence?

Once a current goal is accomplished, it's time to start all over on a new goal – building a life of accomplishment.

STRATEGY 10 – FOLLOW
THESE GUIDELINES FOR SELECTING A BOSS

Your just-out-of-school youngster is not only trying to find the job and company that has the "right fit" but also offers the "right person who will be my direct supervisor."

In fact, the boss your young person chooses can have a significant impact on his or her chances of getting hired in the first place, of doing well on that first job and of effectively managing a career over the long term.

Here's why choosing a "first boss" after considering several entry level jobs is so critical:

- **Chances of being hired** - Hiring managers employ people who are attractive to them -- people they "like." They often like job candidates who reflect their same orientation and values.

- **Subsequent job performance** - If a new employee and supervisor have a similar orientation and values, they are more likely to enjoy working together and to achieve corporate goals more easily with less stress.

- **Career growth** - An effective boss is probably going to be promoted and grow in his or her own career, and your son or daughter will likely have opportunities to piggyback on that success. Those who are promoted often bring key members of their teams with them, especially those who have joined them through entry level jobs.

So, what qualities should your new job finder with special needs require of a new boss, even if he or she is considering entry level jobs, which are often turn out to be short-term?

Here are seven attributes I'd want in a boss, if I were seeking meaningful work in today's job market: *social intelligence, personal optimism, service orientation, tolerance, resilience, focus and restraint.*

Let me give you a little more detail about each attribute.

Social Intelligence

Social intelligence is more than learning how to live with delayed gratification. That's the quick definition I've had in the back of my mind for the last three years.

In fact, social intelligence is not a single skill but a combination of skills, all of which result in being able to teach and be taught, lead and be led and receive and give, says Cynthia Kivland, co-founder and president of Workplace Coach Institute and president of Smart2Smafrter, a coaching and career service firm.

Personal Optimism

But, according to Kivland, optimism (and the curiosity which feeds it) is the one driving force for social intelligence, and so I would want a boss who could attract people through his or her optimism.

I want a supervisor who feels he or she has the power to master destiny by defining perceptions and then checking reality on a continual basis against those personal perceptions. After all, what we all think of as "truth" shifts with time and experience. For me, then, hope is based on experimentation, evolving capabilities, acceptance, persistence, possibility thinking, problem solving and resilience.

As a result, I can let go of the embarrassment of being different or wrong from someone else's perspective -- a freedom that has helped me learn to live well with a disability.

Service Orientation

I want a boss who seeks to build a personal legacy throughout his or her career by striving to be the best *for* the world, not necessarily the best *in* the world. What story does my boss want others to tell about after he or she is gone? Is it one of personal aggrandizement or one of personal service?

Personal service translates into everyday interactions with others. When I say or do things to increase the positive emotions of others, I also increase my positive emotions. When I decrease the positive emotions of others, I diminish myself.

Demagogues divide us for personal gain. A huckster uses aggressive or questionable methods to get his or her way. But, "honest statesmanship is the wise employment of individual manners for the public good," according to Abraham Lincoln.

I think statesmanship is needed on the job, too.

Every member of a work team can have a positive or negative impact within a workplace, but the supervisor in charge sets the tone. I want a supervisor who knows how to use on-the-job statesmanship -- to give instead of receive.

Tolerance

"Tolerance is being empathetic with people you don't want to be empathetic with," admits Kivland in her explanation of social intelligence. Tolerance can most welcome in entry level jobs where "newbies" often make mistakes.

And, I find that attribute particularly helpful due to my disability. I find, especially as I get older, that my disability tends to mask what is authentically positive in me and that my disability highlights my not-disability-related weaknesses. Having a supervisor who is capable of looking beyond disability is a benefit without measure.

Resilience

I show my resilience by continually reinventing how to get things done. Resilience is not necessarily how I initially react to adverse events but how I eventually react and how I navigate the transition. It's what, for example, I tell myself about my disability -- that disability doesn't have to ruin my life.

Like a rubber band, I bounce back from occasional "bad" situations, but, being human, I don't always go back to normal. And, I can admit that.

I expect a similar kind of resilience from my future supervisor.

Focus

I want my supervisor to demonstrate that he or she knows people can evolve, innovate and improve. I try to make five positive comments for every negative comment I make to others, and I would like my supervisor to do the same.

Focus first on what others do right. That's an old Dale Carnegie principle.

Restraint

On the whole, I try to minimize old, not-constructive memories and replace them with new, constructive images, which I can call up in three to six seconds when faced with internal or external events that can throw me off track. I try to stay in the present. I ask questions.

In other words, I try to show restraint and behave calmly in stressful situations. I work at choosing how I want to respond to stress instead of being on auto-pilot and blow off steam. I do that by trying to uncover why I choose to respond the way I do in specific instances.

As a result, I can continually grow in mastering my destiny and focus on outcomes by discovering new thoughts, beliefs, perceptions and responses while working in a variety of entry level jobs. I have a growing understanding of how to help others feel and be great. I'm not a toxic person -- which is good because the combination of toxicity and disability is deadly.

Again, this type of behavior is what I would expect from my supervisor in any entry level job.

But, in reviewing these seven key attributes for an effective supervisor, I've also uncovered this additional insight: I need these same qualities as a job candidate in order to attract the potential supervisor I seek and to be in a position to choose work from a range of entry level jobs. For me, that discovery gives me more confidence as I seek to find a job.

STRATEGY 11 – ARTICULATE A PERSONAL LEADERSHIP PHILOSOPHY

Let me introduce you to Sue, who, I believe, has invested some time in developing her personal leadership philosophy.

Sue is 36, has a master's degree in public administration. She works as a facilitator, recording secretary and strategist on short-term projects for various municipal, county and state government agencies in Missouri.

She also happens to have a disability, uses a power wheelchair and hires personal assistants through a local agency so she can live independently in a downtown apartment in Springfield.

Sue knows how to help small groups clarify their goals and develop strategies which help them achieve those goals. She's a leader in the community because she helps people identify opportunities in which they can excel.

Part of Sue's success is that she also has articulated who she is as a leader, what her personal values are and how she intends to behave and interact with others. In other words, she has developed and articulated a personal leadership philosophy.

In the process, she has become a community leader.

Sue says, "I've learned how to be a leader because I continually have to get multiple personal tasks done on a daily basis – sometimes through a variety of people."

Her family and friends will tell you that making the most of the opportunity to live independently is Sue's passion. Everyone around her knows that because she's a "predictable" leader. She knows what she needs in terms of personal care and she makes it clear to others what she needs and expects.

As a result, her "team" becomes comfortable helping her to meet those needs because they view Sue as a consistent leader. Sue trusts her team members, and they trust her. That approach in her personal life also carries over to the relationships she has formed in her pubic administration work.

Benefits of Having a Leadership Philosophy

Mike Figliuolo, author of "One Piece of Paper: The Simple Approach to Powerful, Personal Leadership," says one of the key benefits of developing a personal leadership philosophy is the trust you can gain from a new boss and a new set of coworkers.

He writes that your new job seeker's consistent behavior, based on personal maxims he or she has developed about how to interact with others, helps your son or daughter become:

- A more decisive leader.
- A more predictable leader.
- A more productive leader.

Your new job seeker needs to be clear about what he or she expects from a boss, coworkers, customers, or suppliers, he explains. If that's not clear, your son or daughter is not going to do good work – no matter where the job title lands on an organization chart.

"If you're clear about your expectations, people will know where you stand. In a leadership position, people may quit on you and pursue other dreams, but that's OK," Figliuolo tells his clients, "because individuals need to find their 'best fit' and ultimately that will improve your own productivity as a leader.

Four Aspects of Leadership

As founder and managing director of ThoughtLeaders, LLC, Figliuolo coaches his clients in developing what he calls a "holistic leadership approach." He helps individuals develop personal maxims for these four aspects of leadership:

- **Leading yourself** – How do you intend to shape your future based on your values, goals, ethics and standards for yourself? How do you bounce back from setbacks? What standards do you set for yourself?
- **Leading the "thinking"** – What are your standards for your team based on your company's compelling vision? How do you foresee the future in terms of risks and opportunities? How do you drive action within your team?
- **Leading your people** – What's your "natural" style for building authentic relationships with the individuals with whom you work? How do you motivate them? How do you stay connected with their "reality?" How do you commit to fostering their personal growth and invest in their development?
- **Leading a balanced life** – How do you keep things in perspective when your team experiences stress? How do you define your personal boundaries and coach others in defining their boundaries?

I have a hunch Sue may have read Figliuolo's book because she has apparently become her own expert at developing self-knowledge.

The key, Figliuolo writes, to developing an authentic leadership philosophy is to recall, record and share with others personal-experience stories about your leadership approaches that allow you to "get out of your head" and into "your gut."

He says you'll then become "authentic" (be your "natural self") in your approach to leadership and be able to record a meaningful series of leadership maxims, which together are no more than a page long but represent your leadership philosophy.

In short, your job seeker's trigger for developing a personal leadership philosophy is recalling and retelling personal stories about instances when he or she demonstrated leadership and felt good about it.

So, help your new job seeker highlight the leadership experience he or she already has (from leading personal assistants and unpaid volunteers to a full-fledged team in a business environment) during upcoming job searches.

Does his or her disability experience naturally lead into a personal leadership philosophy? If so, your new job seeker needs to seize that opportunity (which no one else has) and be prepared to tell why.

At the very least, your young job finder needs to have a one-page handout about his or her personal leadership philosophy handy during job interviews. It may just be the competitive edge your son or daughter needs to outshine job seeker competitors who are not as savvy in describing who they are as leaders.

STRATEGY 12 – BECOME SAVVY
ABOUT WORKPLACE INCLUSION

There are three benchmarks by which your new job seeker can measure the effectiveness of a prospective employer's work diversity record and inclusion efforts.

Of course, many organizations intend to put their diversity values into day-to-day practice so they can effectively integrate qualified people with special needs into their workplaces. But actual practice doesn't always follow intent.

That's why your new job finder needs to become savvy about how workplace inclusion is actually carried out in companies which follow "best practices" in this regard.

As a mentor, you can encourage your new job finder to ask, in his or her mind during second and third interviews for a particular job, these evaluative questions about a prospective employer's diversity practices:

- **Are** the company's statements of mission and values clear and meaningful?

- **How** well is the company communicating that mission and those values?

- **Is** the company actively aligning those values with daily practices?

Clarifying Mission and Values

Encourage your new job finder to ask hiring managers: How did you develop your statements of corporate mission, company values and management philosophy?

The period immediately after corporate-wide disability awareness training is an opportune time for an organization to review its mission and values statements. Look for indications that senior executives as well as a cross section of associates representing every level of the organization had the opportunity to clarify why the organization is in business and what values guide its day-to-day activities.

The resulting statements should be understandable and concrete. Did a representative sampling of people throughout the organization develop a series of specific examples in which each of the firm's value statements about diversity come alive in on-the-job, every-day ways? Only then do an organization's values become guidelines for making day-to-day decisions.

Communicating That Mission and Those Values

Look for a strong corporate communication function within the company – one that helped plan and facilitate the brainstorming sessions for gaining these concrete examples of the organization's values in action.

But corporate communications people should also be in the forefront of summarizing and distributing these concrete examples to the right audiences, using the right media. Are there any indications of an umbrella communication program designed to show what the mission and values mean to individuals at every level of the organization?

Further, are immediate supervisors/contact people fully engaged in interpreting the firm's diversity values into meaningful and useful information for the people they supervise and the customers they serve on a day-to-day basis?

Is that interpretation an ongoing task as work patterns change so those values remain meaningful?

Aligning Those Values with Daily Practices

These immediate supervisors/contact people need to know specifically how the organization's values relate to day-to-day individual practices, team practices and organizational practices. And they need to know how, when and where to communicate that information to the people they supervise.

Here's an outline of the questions supervisors need to answer for the employees they supervise whenever an organization is announcing a policy change, such as a revamped diversity initiative:

- **Why** are we changing, and why it is important to me?
- **What** do you want me to do differently than what I'm doing today? Why?
- **How** will my work be evaluated, and what are the consequences?
- **What** tools and support do I get to make this change?
- **What's** in it for me? What's in it for all of us?

By knowing the answers to those questions, employees know how to effectively carry out the organization's mission, values and philosophy – and can make it easier for your new job finder to transition into a new job and a new organization.

One closing thought: Your new job seeker can gain feedback about a targeted, prospective employer's inclusion efforts by networking on LinkedIn.com with the company's past and present employees, particularly those with special needs. He or she will gain a "leg up" by using the insight from that networking to guide discussions during second and third employment interviews.

STRATEGY 13 – ACQUIRE SOCIAL INTELLIGENCE

What employers typically seek in a job candidate is "social intelligence," according to Cynthia Kivland, MCC, co-founder and president of Workplace Coach Institute and president of Smart2Smarter, a coaching and career service firm.

Social intelligence is more than learning how to live with delayed gratification (the most common definition we often hear for the term, "emotional intelligence"), says Kivland, who has dedicated much of her training efforts to showing the importance of interpersonal communication.

She claims social intelligence is not a single skill but a combination of these skills:

- **Knowing** how to draw upon your self-confidence.
- **Mastering** your emotions and actions.
- **Attracting** other people to you.
- **Being** adaptable and resilient.
- **Showing** tolerance and acceptance.
- **Evolving** and improving emotionally, psychologically and spiritually.
- **Being** able to teach and be taught, lead and be led and receive and give.

These seven skills show the importance of interpersonal communication for your son or daughter with special needs who is entering the "real-world" job market for the first time. Kivland says the seven social intelligence skills she has identified have a common denominator: optimism.

I believe optimism is important for job seekers with special needs because:

- **We tend** to attract people through our optimism. And those people we attract tend to be optimistic, too.
- **We show** our resilience by continually reinventing how to get things done. Resilience does not mean how we initially react to adverse events but how we eventually react -- how we navigate the transition. For example, what we tell ourselves about our disabilities -- that disability doesn't have to ruin the rest of our lives -- is an example of our resilience. Like a rubber band, we're elastic. We bounce back -- even though we may not always bounce back to normal.
- **We demonstrate** that human beings can evolve, innovate and improve -- and that disability does not have to evoke pity or false admiration.

I also believe it's important to avoid coming across to others as a "toxic" person, someone who is mired in old memories, fears and resentments. Together, toxicity and disability are a deadly mix.

On the other hand, one easy way your job seeker can demonstrate elasticity (and social intelligence) is to ask his or her second interviewers for a particular job: "What was it about me that prompted you to call me back for this second job interview?"

By doing so, your son or daughter is showing that, "I can step outside of myself, and I believe I'm capable of mastering my destiny. I can shift my focus and check the reality of my perceptions."

Kivland calls that orientation "hope behavior."

"Hope behavior is based on experimentation, evolving capabilities, acceptance, persistence, possibility thinking, solution orientation, and resilience," advises Kivland. "Let go of the embarrassment of being different or wrong from someone else's perspective."

That's particularly meaningful for me as I continue to struggle, as a senior with greying hair and lifelong disability, to maintain my self-esteem in new situations which call attention to my vulnerabilities.

So, consider Kivland's advice about the importance of social intelligence for your new job seeker with special needs: "Show restraint. Behave calmly in stressful situations. Choose how you want to respond to stress instead of being on auto-pilot. Discover why you choose to respond the way you do."

Kivland also adds this: "You'll soon find yourself mastering your destiny and focusing on outcomes instead of the past. You'll discover new thoughts, beliefs, perceptions and responses. You'll have an understanding of how to help others be great. As a result, you'll be an attractive job candidate -- one who is striving to be the best *for* the world (instead of the best *in* the world)."

That can be your young job finder's disability edge.

STRATEGY 14 – FRAME DISABILITY FROM A DISABILITY PERSPETIVE

For years, I've been grappling with ways to show hiring managers that the attributes I've acquired in effectively handling the various aspects of disability make me a job candidate they need to seriously consider in their hiring decisions.

I now know I was searching for a series of attributes that individuals need to effectively tap in order to authentically communicate with their potential bosses.

In September 2011, I attended a "Dealing with Trauma" presentation author and speaker Gary Karp made to a group of graduate students who were studying to be physical therapists at the University of Wisconsin-Madison. Since then, I've been making notes about how I would guide recent college graduates with special needs who are now in the market for jobs. How can they come up with their own "disability frame of reference" as they prepare for their entry into the job market?

Thank you, Gary, for sparking my interest in helping people with special needs define what disability means to them and identifying some of these attributes for the individuals who coach them.

Seven Ways to Frame Disability

Here are the essential attributes I have so far: adaptability, self-confidence, self-advocacy, potential, freedom, self-determination and gratification – communication platforms I would suggest new job seekers with special needs consider as they develop their job marketing programs.

Please massage and add and substrate as you, in coaching your son or daughter, see fit. I'm the first to admit that these seven ways to frame disability are always in the process of "becoming."

Adaptability

Like most students (with and without a disability), you most likely will find for yourself that you are capable of going beyond of what you first imagine you can do. In fact, you may find yourself eventually doing what you first thought was impossible. And, you may discover what it's like to be what people like to call "courageous," which most commonly means facing a difficulty without fear.

What you'll more likely discover is that courage is actually learning how to handle fear so you'll be able to figure out how to work around your disability. In other words, people in general are very adaptable. You are living proof of that bit of good news, and you'll be surprised how friends, acquaintances and strangers will be genuinely grateful to you for simply being a living example of that good news.

Remember that you are neither "heroic" nor "pathetic" as a person with special needs. In dealing with your disability, you'll probably fall somewhere in the middle of those two extremes: simply "effective" or "adaptive." Shun "tragic" or "inspirational" as descriptors of your situation in life.

In my own case, I learned that illustrating adaptability was one of my key opportunities while at work. For example, I learned how to delegate authority early in my career to people reporting directly to me as well as to co-workers who could benefit from a little increased responsibility, visibility and recognition.

I took courses about how to delegate well and found that effective delegation not only strengthened my team but also demonstrated my people management skills to my superiors and coworkers, who became less reluctant to delegate effectively in their own jobs. It was one of the key reasons I became a vice president, even though I had a disability and walked and talked with difficulty.

Self-confidence

Encourage others to be honest about your disability by showing them you can handle honesty about yourself and your capabilities as well as your limitations.

Anger, denial, and depression are all natural ways of coping with both a lifelong and acquired disability, but still using your disability as a scapegoat along your journey toward acceptance of your personal vulnerabilities is a distraction. It hinders the development of your self-confidence.

I have found that showing self-confidence has been one of my most important attributes.

I credit my mom with showing me that dwelling on what I could not change in terms of my capability was a waste of time. Instead, even in grade school, I concentrated on what I thought was possible: learning shorthand so I could take notes, learning to use the keyboard etc.

Those little successes helped me build my self-confidence and eventually work around obstacles I, at first, thought I could not overcome.

Self-advocacy

In today's society, you need to advocate for yourself as a person with special needs. No one will do it for you (or at least as good as you can do it for yourself).

Again, my mother modeled what self-advocacy could become for me. I flunked first grade in a rural, one-room school house, so she taught me first grade herself. Then, she found her way around state government service offerings and gained help from key people in various agencies for placing me in an orthopedic grade school 60 miles from our home farm.

That break-through put me on the path to independence.

Potential

Remember to be kind to yourself. How you want to handle your disability may not always be how you actually react to it in real life, and that's acceptable. After all, you're human. Your failures, though, show you what is possible in your life. They reveal your potential.

As a person with special needs, you learn to celebrate what is possible instead of what you never had or what you lost and once had. Continually mourning an incapability or a loss is like dragging around old baggage. It's actually a pathology not associated with your disability.

Even in sixth grade, I knew I wanted to be a writer. But, I remember long nights when I had a theme to write for a next-day high school class and was writing it laboriously in long-hand because I didn't yet know how to use a manual typewriter.

But, it was just a matter of taking one step at a time to become a writer. Those steps included going to a "regular" high school back home, finding an accessible college which offered journalism, getting good grades, finding my niche in the real work world etc.

Freedom

You are not "confined" by your disability but can feel "liberated" by assistive technology that, for instance, provides power chairs for mobility, tablets for quick access to the Internet and Communication Access Real-time Translation for hearing. That's a type of freedom.

You know that assistive technology has not advanced to the point where you can instantly disappear in one room and reappear in another, so you don't have to dwell on that possibility and how convenient and cool that would be. It's not yet possible. You don't miss it because you can't do it. That's another kind of freedom.

So, you don't dwell on what is not possible and what you don't miss. Instead, you focus on real possibilities. Getting that concept across to people without a disability is sometimes difficult, but it's another key concept that can become real for you.

Assistive technology can be relatively simple. At least, it was in the 1960s. One of my first liberating moments occurred when I started college and mobility between classes became an important issue for me.

I always enjoyed providing the motor power for classmates who used wheelchairs while in grade school because the wheelchair also gave me stability and balance. So, I bought a grocery cart from a local supermarket, placed my books inside the cart and started pushing it between classes at college, leaving it outside (rain or shine) each building while I attended classes inside.

I tagged the cart with this sign: "This is the property of Jim Hasse. Please do not move." It was always there when my classes were done and I needed it to get back to my dorm.

That was one my first successes in becoming a communicator.

Self-determination

Treasure people and situations which offer you options because choices, such as the option of obtaining the type of help when you need it on your own terms, is the hallmark of self-determination and independence.

Gaining an understanding from others about what self-determination means to you is often difficult. I'm forever grateful to my employer of 29 years for refusing to limit me to work what others would usually assume I could and could not do.

Gratification

Document the skills you learn from living well with a disability and practice telling stories about how you developed them and how they relate to the workplace. Those anecdotes will come in handy for showing prospective employers how your disability experience has prepared you for enhancing their bottom lines.

In doing so, you may discover that you are surprisingly gratified by the unusual opportunities you've had because of your disability experience.

I know I wouldn't be the person I am today without my experiences of battling (and thriving) with my disability. Through the people I met while attending my orthopedic grade school, for instance, I've had the opportunity to travel in Africa, Russia and Europe.

Summarizing my Disability Framework

So, after thinking about this series of attributes and personalizing it for my own benefit, here's how I would put my disability into a context for todays' prospective employers.

> **"By learning to live well with my disability, I have learned how to work around obstacles.**
>
> **"Creating my own work-around solutions to real as well as perceived problems has strengthened my adaptability, my self-confidence, my self-determination and my independence – attributes that make me a team player as well as an innovator."**

What You Can Do as a Mentor

You can go through the same exercise with the job finder you are mentoring. Help your young man or woman with special needs build his or her own framework for disability based on personal experience.

Your job seeker needs to personalize his or her disability frame of reference and then use it as a competitive advantage in today's job market.

Encourage your young adult to tell prospective hiring managers stories about how he or she can work with "disability savvy" and contribute to the bottom line.

STRATEGY 15 – CONCENTRATE ON PRODUCTIVTTY

Knowing how to work less but do more can be a career builder for your mature son or daughter who has special needs and is now entering the job market. It can help him or her get hired. Let me explain.

Yes, job seeking is a full-time job. But, no, it does not have to consume the life of your son or daughter who is making the transition from school to work. Gaining that balance is knowing how to set and achieve goals.

In fact, learning how to work less and still get more done than competitors for a particular job before working full-time is a valuable skill your son or daughter can highlight in the bundle of personal attributes he or she markets to prospective employers.

Those who are productive in their job searches are likely to be productive on the job. Employers are well aware of that fact. And, knowing how to effectively manage personal time may be even more important for your youngster with special needs. Prospective hiring managers, after all, probably wonder in their heads whether, as a result of disability, your son or daughter will be able "to carry their share of the load" within a work setting.

Work Less, Do More

That's why I'm particularly impressed with what Stever Robbins, a recognized time management expert and executive, has to say about maximizing productivity on the job without sacrificing one's personal life.

He's a graduate of Harvard Business School and MIT. His newest book is "Get-It-Done Guy's Nine Steps to Work Less and Do More."

I like Robbins' basic premise about productivity. He believes putting in eight hours of work a day is irrelevant (particularly for the person who is self-employed). What counts is working on activities which have the most impact on achieving one's most important goals. He recommends spending time on what will move a project forward toward those goals. Again -- a mature approach to goal setting.

Robbins says goal setting needs to give direction to one's life. Goals can help your son or daughter develop the kind of life he or she wants.

So, he recommends, "First, decide how you want to spend your time --- and then set goals which control your time and which will help you achieve that kind of life."

Nine Productivity Steps

In his book, Robbins gives a broad range of quick tips for managing time effectively. I'd like to share a few of them with you that I find refreshing and that you may want to pass on to your job seeker with special needs. I'll do that in the context of his nine productivity steps.

His nine steps to working less and doing more are:

1. **Live on purpose.** Live the life you want. Write down your primary goals and review them regularly out loud (daily). Then, as you go about your work, ask yourself, "Why am I doing this task?"
2. **Stop procrastination.** Make a commitment to other people (perhaps through a mastermind group) to get work done and then set aside "action days" to do it.
3. **Conquer technology.** Technology today increases our productivity, but it can also be a burden because it gets in the way sometimes of getting things done. Technology doesn't always make our lives better. It can be a time waster and a

distraction. So, do a "technology audit" by writing down what you use and how it helps you with your purpose.

4. **Stop distractions.** Staying focused is difficult today. Your computer is a tool, not a "place." Put a "to do" sticky note on your computer screen, complete those tasks and then take the note off. That frees you to do other non-computer tasks.

5. **Optimize.** Examine the ways you get things done every four to six months. How can you complete a task with the least time and effort?

6. **Stay organized.** "Messy" is not always bad, if you can find what you need, but searching for something and not being able to find it is a time waster. Everything needs a place. Before you clean your desk, categorize your "stuff" first on paper and then move things that are on your list.

7. **Stop wasting time.** Don't try to open and answer every e-mail, for instance. Getting your e-mail inbox to zero is a time waster.

8. **Build stronger relationships.** Most of business today is based on relationships. With effective relationships, you can ask for favors, get a little slack, make and receive more referrals, and have more reach.

9. **Leverage.** Look for ways to multiply your results without more time on your part through delegation, subcontracting, repurposing etc. Do what you do best and arrange for others to help you with tasks that are not in your top-skill range. Make rules for the decisions you need to make on a routine basis so you don't have to consider every option every time (such as deciding which e-mail to open).

Robbins defines productivity as how much work it takes to get the results you want from your job and to live your life to the fullest. He says that means sometimes you need to say "no" to someone who is seeking a portion of your time.

I wish I had these bits of advice 50 years ago. I was 20 and needed advice about goal setting for adults.

The key concept in goal setting is that people can be in charge of their lives. Your son or daughter needs to decide how he or she will use personal time (and let no one else make that decision).

In doing so, your young job finder will be able to answer, in concrete and convincing terms, the often-unasked question in job interviews: "With your disability, how do you intend to carry your share of the weight in this job?" That skeptical question can be turned into an opportunity to offer examples of "how I've learned to make the best use of my time."

STRATEGY 16 – LEARN
HOW TO APPROACH SALARY, BENEFIT
NEGOTIATIONS

Salary and benefits are not always cast in stone, especially if the job is beyond the entry level.

But, even at the entry level, your job finder needs to remember that he or she is always a "seller" -- not a "buyer." Even after being offered a job, it's important that he or she retains that "selling" mindset.

Prospective employers are "buyers." After all, a hiring manager does not "give" an applicant a job. A successful job candidate "earns" it because, based on skills, attributes and experience, he or she is the best candidate for the job in the eyes of the hiring manager.

In other words, your young job finder has "value" -- which may come as a surprise to you both because disability can lead to feelings of being "discounted" in other situations (recreation opportunities, romantic relationships etc.) because of it.

In many cases, negotiating salary and benefits is like being a street vendor in Nairobi. Your job finder has a fine piece of linen to sell. A shopper stops and is looking for a bargain. That shopper has a maximum amount he or she will pay. Your job finder has a minimum price at which he or she will sell.

Like any other merchant, your son or daughter needs to know what "price" to set, in his or her own mind, for the product -- in this case, his or her skills, attributes, temperament and experience as an employee. That's when a salary calculator comes in handy. And, then, the next step is to negotiate for it, if the "price" offered is out of line with the market and the kind of product being sold.

But, what is a person worth as an employee? Like the price of any other product, what salary and benefits a job seeker gets is determined by a number of factors – not just the results of an online salary calculator.

When a strict salary and benefit structure is not in place, here are four questions your job seeker can ask him or herself before deciding how far to press an employer about salary and benefit issues after a job offer has been received.

- **What is** the job worth in the marketplace?
- **What does** the employer really need?
- **How well** do I meet those employer needs?
- **Do I know** how to negotiate effectively?

Now is the time to pass this four-cornered salary calculator on to your new job seeker. Here is more detail:

What is the Job Worth in the Marketplace?

You can get a good idea about the appropriate salary range for the job you've just been offered by using a combination of these tools:

- Salary.com's free Salary Wizard, which is an actual online salary calculator.
- The current Occupational Outlook Handbook by the U.S. Department of Labor.
- Career placement services.
- Online networking and in-person informational interviews.
- Professional associations.

Study the Occupational Outlook Handbook closely for trends in jobs which are increasing in demand and those which are decreasing in demand. Where does the job you've just been offered fall?

That will give you some idea of what kind of "wiggle room" you have when you're negotiating your salary and benefits. Jobs with short supply offer more opportunity for negotiation than jobs which have static or falling demand.

What Does the Employer Really Need?

Even if the job you've just been offered is not in high demand, *you* can be. At this point, hopefully, you've done your research and know as much about the company as you can. You know what your hiring manager realizes he needs as well as, perhaps, his unrealized needs.

And, you've done a good bit of work in showing how what you offer matches his needs -- especially the needs that he believes are most critical.

How Well Do I Meet those Employer Needs?

Does your new hiring manager really need someone with online marketing expertise or heavyweight contacts within the publishing industry or first-hand experience in the landscaping business for high-end homeowners?

If your expertise goes beyond the minimum qualifications for the job you're offered and you've been able to show how your expertise can fill a previously unrecognized hole, you're in a good position to negotiate a compensation deal that goes beyond what was in the initial job announcement.

If, however, in the eyes of your new hiring manager, you appear to be qualified, trainable but not yet seasoned in the disciplines which really count within the company, you're probably not in a good position to negotiate salary and benefits beyond what was first slated for the job.

Do I Know How to Negotiate Effectively?

But, if you're satisfied with your responses to those first three questions I've posed, then you're ready to negotiate with your new employer about your salary and benefits.

First, let's consider what is relevant (and what is not) in such negotiations. In general, your needs -- or even your wants -- are not the basis for your worth as a worker in the eyes of an employer. But, location can be. After all, there can be quite a difference in living expenses between a job in Manhattan, Kansas, and one in Manhattan, New York City. Rely on online salary calculator resources for getting a picture of differences in living expenses by location.

Second, what you were paid in the past is not what you are worth now for a particular job.

"It shouldn't matter what you were making at your last job, especially in a world where 17-year-olds who were earning five bucks an hour flipping burgers last year are earning $40k this year designing web pages and where $100k executives are seeking $50k sales jobs," writes Nick Corcodilos, host of asktheheadhunter.com.

If an employer tries to get you to say what you've been making, use it as an opportunity to showcase your diplomatic skills. Steer the conversation back to the value of the job to the company (and specifically to your hiring manager).

Third, your disability is not relevant. By the time you're discussing salary and benefits of a job, you should have eliminated the impact of your disability on such negotiations.

Don't wait for the employer to bring up the topic of salary and benefits, but don't put your expectations in your résumé or cover letter or in a conversation that is not part of the negotiation process. Instead, put on your "negotiator" hat before the negotiation process begins and think about what you want, what your hiring manager wants, and how you can persuade him or her to come around to your way of thinking.

What are the important issues to negotiate? Salary? Other benefits? Accommodations? Opportunities for advancement? You need to know what you want, but your hiring manager also needs to know what he or she has to offer.

In short, are you looking at the negotiation from the employer's point of view as much or more than your own? That's vital.

Most of all, be persuasive, be realistic, be open, be flexible, be articulate and be prepared. And be ready to learn from the result so you can be better prepared in future negotiations. In doing so, you've become your own best salary calculator.

Many new job finders who are just out of school have little insight about how to negotiate effectively for salary and benefits. Knowing about the do's and don't's of negotiation can be your new job finder's competitive edge.

SUMMARY

Preparing for a meaningful career as a new job finder with special needs can seem overwhelming at times. But, as a career-coaching parent, you can help your youngster to do just that by focusing on these key strategies:

Growing in Self-confidence

Strategy 1: Recognize the Importance of Motivation - Your job finder can demonstrate personal motivation and self-confidence during job interviews by being savvy (and helpful) about the on-the-job accommodations he or she needs.

Strategy 2: Concentrate on Four Basic Skills - There are essentially four basic skills which can determine how successful a job candidate will be in landing a meaningful job. Those four basic skills are: marketing, advocating, problem solving and negotiating.

Strategy 3: Build a Personal Brand - Building a personal brand is essential in today's job market. Doing so takes time. But, it's worth the effort because it's a confidence booster.

Strategy 4: Consider a Functional Resume - A functional resume is particularly useful for emphasizing transferrable skills from volunteer or paid work or coursework for those who are new graduates and who have limited experience.

Strategy 5: Develop a "Good Answer" for Job Interviews - By developing a "good answer" to show disability can be a strength instead of a weakness, your young job seeker can minimize fear of job interviews and exhibit more self-confidence because he or she will begin to see the whole job search process in a more positive light.

Strategy 6: Prepare for Tricky Job Interview Questions - There are many job interview questions that are potential "job killers" for your new job finder, but, in most cases, such difficulties can be avoided through company research, personal branding and interview practice.

Strategy 7: Make the Most of These Three Career Builders - Based on my personal experience, I'd rank these three topics near the top of my "critical things to do," if I were about to make the big transition from school to work: networking effectively, targeting companies and dressing well.

Strategy 8: Network within Targeted Companies - Your new job seeker needs to learn how to effectively build a network of contacts within targeted companies – contacts who represent an informal online job market because they are the first to know about new openings within their workplaces.

Strategy 9: Use this Personal Development Template - Encourage your son or daughter to form a "mastermind" group of three to four people in which each participant can face each other, preferably in person, and collaborate on finding answers to key questions related to a job search.

Strategy 10: Follow these Guidelines for Selecting a Boss - The boss your young person chooses can have a significant impact on his or her chances of getting hired in the first place, of doing well on that first job and of effectively managing a career over the long term.

Discovering Disability's Competitive Advantage

Strategy 11: Articulate a Personal Leadership Philosophy - Your young job finder needs to have a one-page handout about his or her personal leadership philosophy handy during job interviews. It may just be the competitive edge your son or daughter needs to outshine job seeker competitors who are not as savvy in describing who they are as leaders.

Strategy 12: Become Savvy about Workplace Inclusion - There are three benchmarks by which your new job seeker can measure the effectiveness of a prospective employer's work diversity record and inclusion efforts.

Strategy 13: Acquire Social Intelligence - These seven social intelligence skills have a common denominator: optimism.

Strategy 14: Frame Disability from a Positive Perspective - Your job seeker needs to personalize his or her disability frame of reference and then use it as a competitive advantage in today's job market. Encourage your young adult to tell prospective hiring managers stories about how he or she can work with "disability savvy" and contribute to the bottom line.

Strategy 15: - Concentrate on Productivity - Knowing how to work less but do more can be a career builder for your mature son or daughter who has special needs and is now entering the job market. It can help him or her get hired.

Strategy 16: Learn How to Approach Salary, Benefit Negotiations - Even at the entry level, your job finder needs to remember that he or she is always a "seller" -- not a "buyer." Even after being offered a job, it's important that he or she retains that "selling" mindset.

I wish you much success in working with your new job finder on these 16 key career-building strategies.

NATIONAL CAREER DEVELOPMENT
GUIDELINES

According to the National Career Development Guidelines (NCDG), these are the career development competencies your job finder young person should possess at the "implementation" level while making the school-to-work transition:

- *Valuing* one's personal interests, likes, and dislikes as a step toward building and maintaining a positive **self-concept**.

- *Practicing* respect for **diversity** as an essential positive interpersonal skill.

- *Anticipating* growth and **change** as essential parts of career development.

- *Achieving* a **balance** among personal, leisure, community, learner, family and work roles.

- *Acting* on the premise that **educational** achievement and performance levels are needed to reach personal and career goals.

- *Committing* to ongoing, **lifetime learning** as a means for enhancing one's ability to function well in a diverse and changing economy.

- *Creating* and managing a **career plan** for meeting career goals.

- *Making* **decisions** within an overall personal strategy for managing a career.

- *Using* accurate, current and unbiased **career information** in planning and managing one's career.

- *Accumulating* consistently the fundamental knowledge about the variety of **skills** (such as communicating, critical thinking, and problem solving) that are important for success and advancement in school and work.

- *Analyzing* changes in employment **trends**, societal needs and economic conditions and the impact they have on one's career path.

LAST THOUGHTS

If they would have known, my college classmates would have said that, after graduation in 1965, I ended up working in the "armpit of Wisconsin," a crossroads with a total population of 187 people who supported three bars and two churches.

But, my story about how I became a vice president for a Fortune 500 company in the 1980s is essentially a narrative about the three attributes I discovered among my coworkers in that tiny town: acceptance, patience and inclusion.

Those characteristics were not mandated by law. After all, the Americans with Disabilities Act (ADA) didn't become law until 1990.

But, three decades ago, in the rural Midwest, those values were not uncommon.

In my case, I started working in my first job out of college for a local dairy cooperative. It was 1965. I had grown up on a dairy farm, worked on 4-H projects, went to a small high school and attended church on Sunday mornings. Most of my coworkers had a similar background.

In 1965, what made me different from my coworkers is that I had a college education and I had CP. Yes, I stuck out as unusual, but that didn't seem to matter much because I was a "farm boy," the general manager of the cooperative (Floyd) knew my family as neighbors, my uncle (Dean) was the cooperative's chief engineer and my boss (Bob) had gone to college with a classmate who also had CP.

As a commodity-focused business which valued financial stability, tangible results and equal treatment for the owners (the farmers who supplied the milk for butter and cheese manufacturing), the cooperative experienced tremendous growth between 1965 and 1995 as the Midwest dairy industry restructured through many mergers and consolidations of local cooperative and privately-owned cheese manufacturing plants.

Automation and technology drove that restructuring. Yet, in 1979, when I became a member of the organization's senior management team, I realized we still basically consisted of grownup "farm boys" who went to Friday-night football games, attended the same churches and preferred buttered crackers as a hors d'oeuvre.

The organization's core values survived the restructuring, allowing me to find my own bearings and prove what I could do within that corporate culture.

As a 70-year-old, I now believe we almost always learn something from each work experience – even in so-called "rotten" jobs, a term I didn't hear very often in the 1960s, which compared to today's sluggish job market, were "pretty good" years.

After graduating from college, my first job was writing and editing "copy." My "desk" was a foldable (and wobbly) card table in the back of the dingy break room where I had all-day access to the coffee pot and an electric "milkhouse heater." I was routinely interrupted by co-workers who were ready for a 15-minute "party."

Many days I was discouraged because I felt caught in a "dead-end" job (and disliked coffee). But I also honed my writing and copy editing skills and learned newsletter layout during those first two years in the break room. It was not a "rotten" job." I now know it was a job which provided the experience I needed.

Even then, I knew it was another small step in my personal quest to build an independent life, admitting that there would likely be many roadblocks to achieving that dream because of CP. I knew, despite the disappointment (I had dreamed about working on Wacker Drive in Chicago as a new college grad) and unpleasantness, that job would eventually be my passport to a meaningful career.

And it did. 20 years later, I ended up as vice president for corporate communication for that same company (now Foremost Farms USA), a position I held for 10 years.

ABOUT JIM HASSE, THE AUTHOR

Jim Hasse is the founder of <u>cerebral-palsy-career-builders.com</u>, the comprehensive career coaching guide for parents of CP youngsters 7 to 27 years old.

He owns Hasse Communication Counseling, LLC, which helps champions of disability employment form partnerships for win-win direct mail fundraisers.

As a Global Career Developmental Facilitator (GCDF) since 2005, he's the author of 12 Amazon eBooks, each of which explains his central premise: that disability, when framed correctly, can be a competitive advantage in today's job market for job seekers with special needs.

To access his books in electronic as well as soft-cover formats, see http://tinyurl.com/JRH-All-Books-Amazon.

Hasse developed an award-winning corporate communication function for Foremost Farms USA, Baraboo, WI, during his service of 29 years at the cooperative -- 10 of which were at the vice presidential level.

Between 1999 and 2009, he was responsible for all the online content of eSight Careers Network, New York City. As eSight's senior content developer, he wrote, assigned and edited more than 1,300 articles about disability employment issues.

Between 1997 and 2001 (before blogging became commonplace), Hasse developed, facilitated and marketed tell-us-your-story.com, a now discontinued web site where people with disabilities shared their personal-experience stories and which provided a launching pad for eSight Careers Network.

A 1965 honors graduate of the University of Wisconsin-Madison's School of Journalism, Hasse is an Accredited Business Communicator (ABC) by the International Association of Business Communicators, San Francisco, Calif.

In 1994, he received the Cooperative Spirit Award from the Cooperative Communicators Association (CCA), a national organization for professional communications employed by cooperatives, and the Cooperative Builder Award from a state-wide association of cooperatives in Wisconsin.

In 1995, he received CCA's H.E. Klinefelter Award for distinguished service in cooperative communications.

In addition to his eBooks and soft-cover books, Hasse is the author of "Break Out: Finding Freedom When You Don't Quite Fit The Mold" (Quixote Press, 1996). a memoir of 51 short stories about disability awareness.

He also compiled and edited "Perfectly Able: How to Attract and Hire Talented People with Disabilities" (AMACOM, 2011), a disability recruitment guidebook for hiring managers that highlights disability's competitive advantage in today's job market.

JIM BOOKS

7TRANSFORMATION
STORIES

Quick Career-insight Series of Seven Little Books
for **Parents of Youngsters with CP**

Each of the seven Little Books takes about 40 minutes to read. Each illustrates and summarizes the essential career builders for your youngster's age group – all through seven transformational stories about Jim Hasse's personal experience as a person with CP.

You'll find considerably more detail about each career builder at <u>cerebral-palsy-career-builders.com,</u> which can be used as an ongoing reference for "how to" information as your youngster matures.

Buy **Little Book 1** on Amazon
at- http://www.amazon.com/dp/B00DPLHRTI

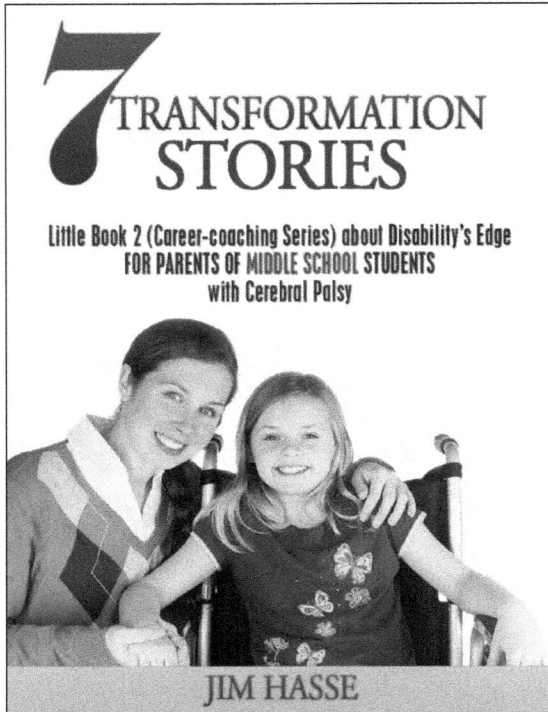

Buy **Little Book 2** on Amazon
at http://www.amazon.com/dp/B00H9WAKHA

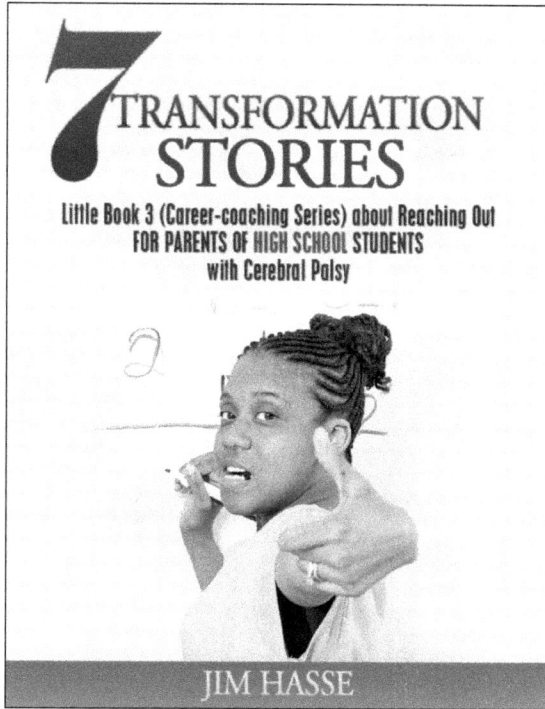

Buy **Little Book 3** on Amazon
at http://www.amazon.com/dp/B00HB77RAQ

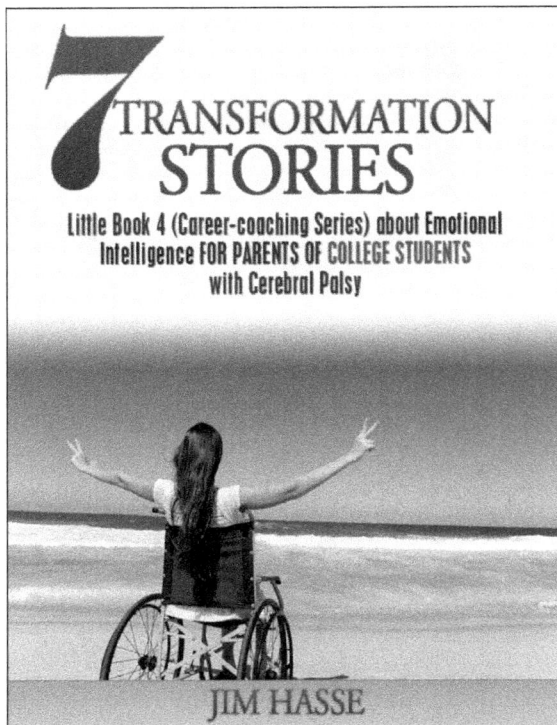

Buy **Little Book 4** on Amazon
at http://www.amazon.com/dp/B00HBDUJ96

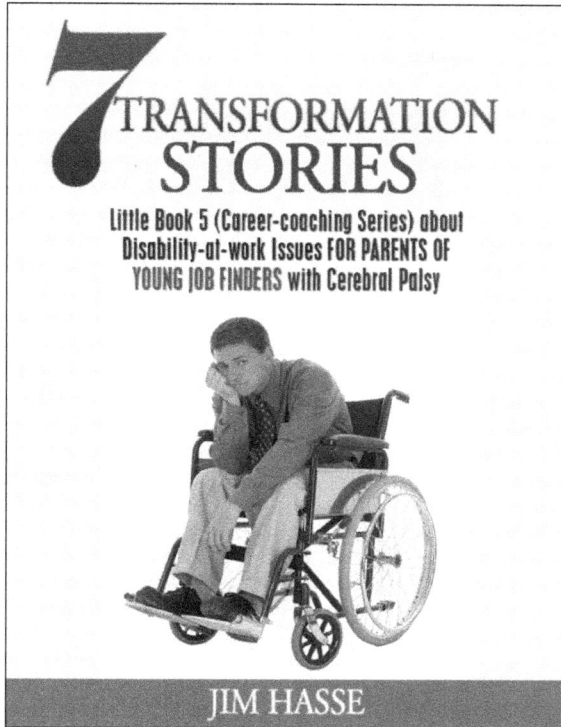

Buy **Little Book 5** on Amazon
at http://www.amazon.com/dp/B00HBVTZ02

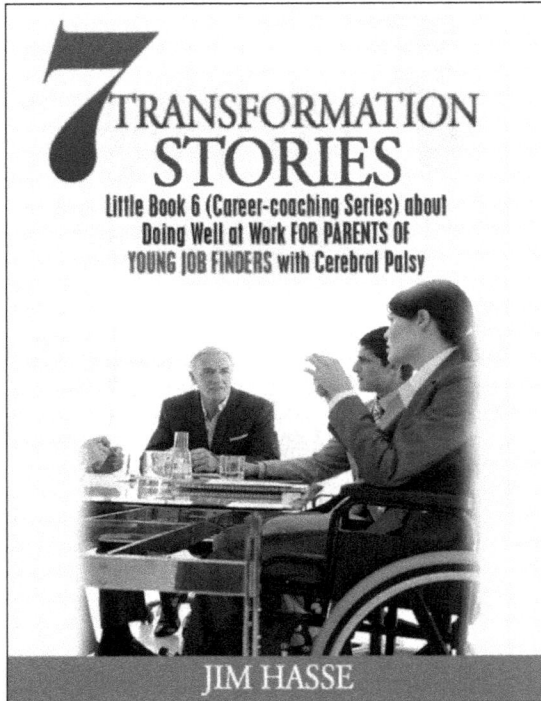

Buy **Little Book 6** on Amazon
at http://www.amazon.com/dp/B00HE60J8G

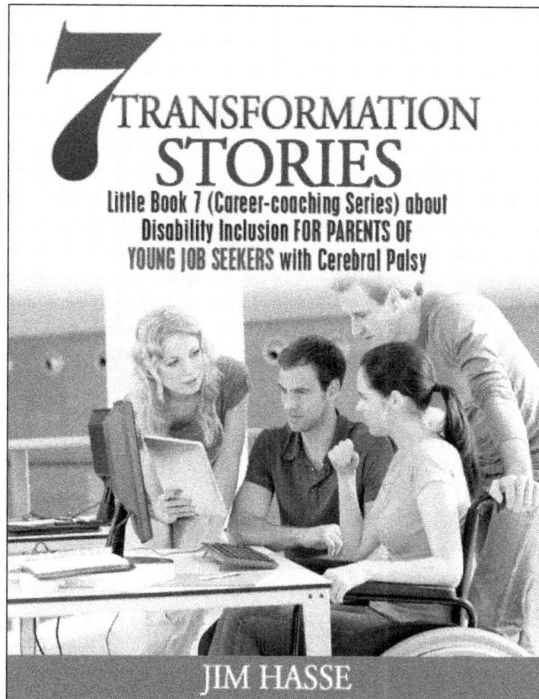

Buy **Little Book 7** on Amazon
at http://www.amazon.com/dp/B00HEVJYUU

Five Books *for* Parenting Youngsters with Special Needs

CAREER BOOK

Each of these five books (available in electronic and paperback formats) takes about 40 minutes to read. Each illustrates and summarizes the essential career development strategies to follow for your youngster's age group – all based on the roadmap recommended by National Career Development Guidelines (NCDG) and Jim Hasse's experience as a Global Career Development Facilitator and as a person with cerebral palsy and mainstream work experience.

You'll find considerably more detail about each career building strategy at www.cerebral-palsy-career-builders.com, which can be used as an ongoing reference for "how to" information as your youngster matures.

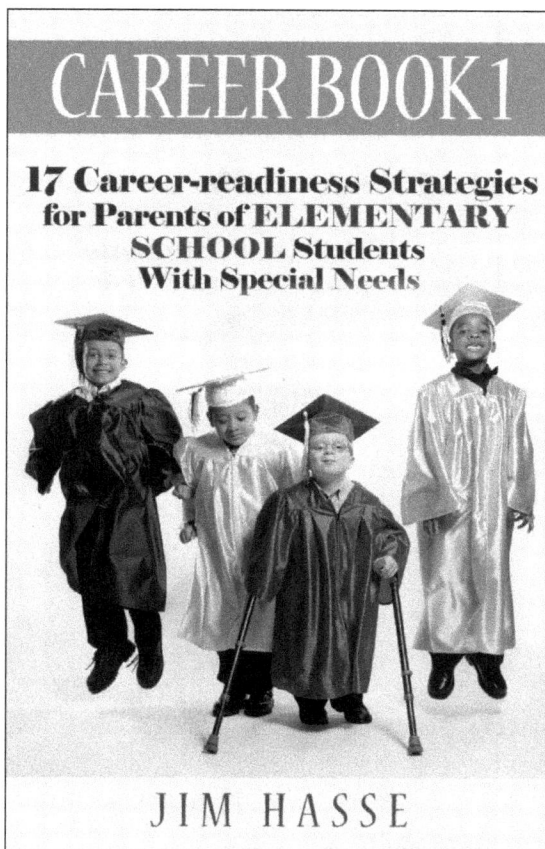

Buy **Career Book 1** on Amazon
at http://www.amazon.com/dp/B00JNYH6JM

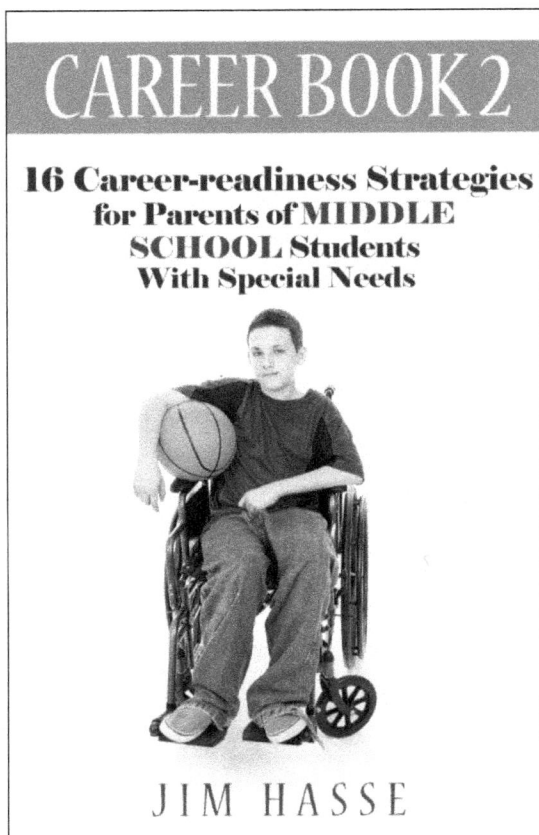

Buy **Career Book 2** on Amazon
at http://www.amazon.com/dp/B00KLIMPBS

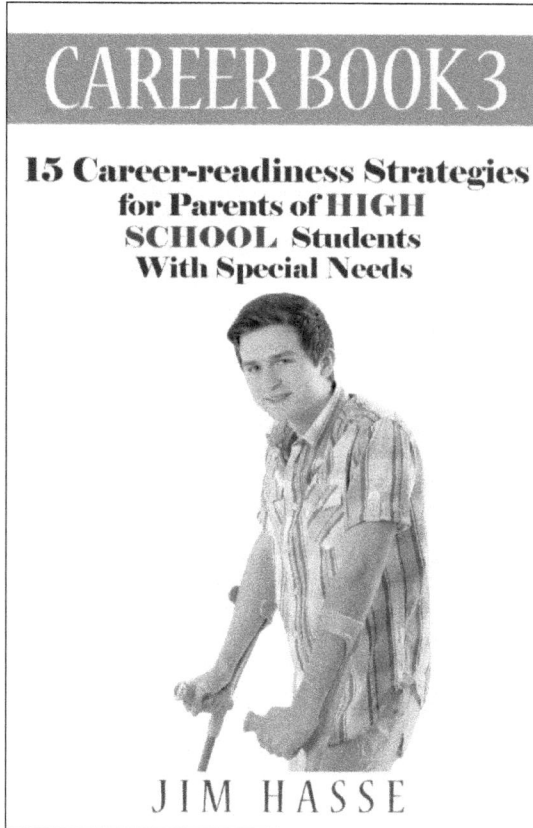

Buy **Career Book 3** on Amazon
at http://www.amazon.com/dp/B00KN2OF56

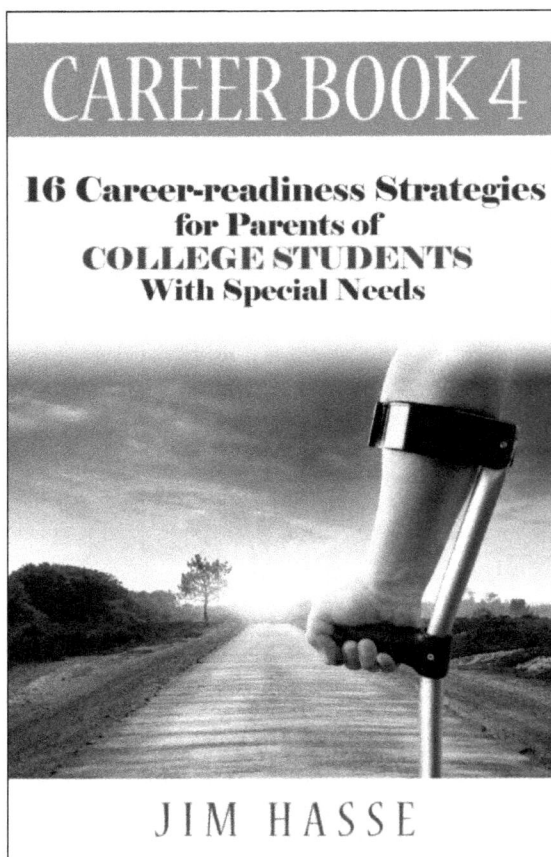

CAREER BOOK 4

16 Career-readiness Strategies
for Parents of
COLLEGE STUDENTS
With Special Needs

JIM HASSE

Buy **Career Book 4** on Amazon
at http://www.amazon.com/dp/B00KPGV5B2

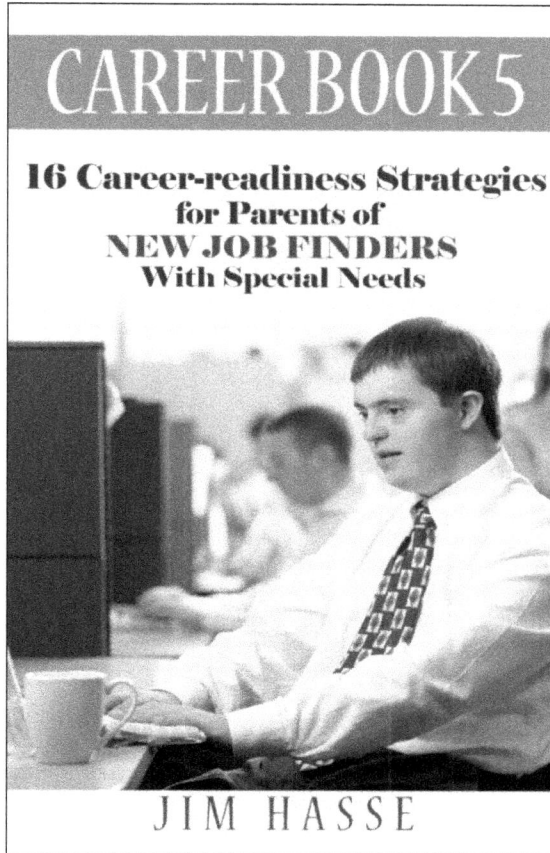

Buy **Career Book 5** on Amazon
at http://www.amazon.com/dp/B00KQRZIHC.

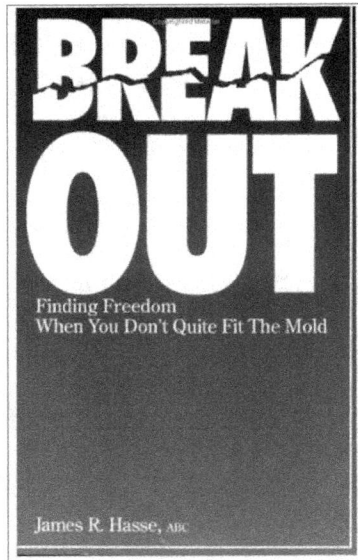

Buy on Amazon at http://tinyurl.com/breakoutjim2
"Break Out: Finding Freedom When You Don't Quite Fit the Mold,"
a memoir of 51 short stories about disability awareness (Quixote Press, 1996).